Jim Abbott

PHOTO CREDITS
Allsport USA
Kevin Levine: Cover. Stephen Dunn: pg. 2, 18 and 26.
Rick Stewart: pg. 6, 25 and 29. Earl Richardson: pg. 9.
Otto Greule, Jr.: pg. 10 and 13. Joe Patronite: pg. 14 and 17.
Tim DeFrisco: pg. 22. Lonnie Major: pg. 30.

Distributed to Schools and Libraries
in the United States by
ENCYCLOPAEDIA BRITANNICA CORP.
310 S. Michigan Avenue
Chicago, Illinois 60604

Library of Congress Catalog-in-Publication Data
Rambeck, Richard
Jim Abbott / Richard Rambeck.
p. cm.
Summary: A biography of the California Angels pitcher who
became the first player to make it to the major leagues with only one hand.
ISBN 1-56766-072-X
1. Abbott, Jim. 1967- –Juvenile literature. 2. Baseball players–United States–
Biography–Juvenile literature. [1. Abbott, Jim, 1967-
2. Baseball players. 3. Physically handicapped.]
I. Title.
GV865.A26R36 1994   92-43044
796.357'092–dc20   CIP/AC
[B]

Jim Abbott

by Richard Rambeck

Abbott is a popular player.

On July 9, 1989, the California Angels hosted the Equitable Old-Timers All-Star Game, which featured former great major-league players. Several of these stars from the past wanted to meet one of the current California Angels pitchers. This pitcher wasn't an all-star, or even a star on his own team. In fact, he was a rookie who had won fewer than ten games in the major leagues. But the former great players wanted to meet Jim Abbott and shake his hand. Abbott, who was only twenty-one years old, was surprised that such great players would want to meet him. "This is incredible," he said.

Two nights before the Old-Timers All-Star Game, Hall of Fame pitcher Warren Spahn dropped by the Angels dugout to say hello to Abbott. On the morning of the game, another Hall of Famer, Bobby Doerr, brought a baseball for Abbott to sign. Then Ernie Banks, yet another Hall of Famer, asked if he could have his picture taken with the young pitcher. As great as these former stars were, they all admired Jim Abbott, who was a lefty. He wasn't the first lefty ever, but he was unusual. Abbott was the first player to make it to the major leagues with only one hand. He had been born with a right arm, but not a right hand.

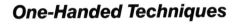
Jim Abbott was born with a disability, but he refused to let it bother him. "This young guy has never once in his life said, 'I wish I had two hands,'" explained his father, Mike Abbott. Young Abbott grew up playing both baseball and football, but baseball was his first love. He learned a way to throw and field with his left hand. When he was throwing the ball, he would rest the glove on the stub of his right arm. After he let go of the ball, he would slide his left hand into the mitt. When he had caught the ball, he would place the glove under his right armpit and quickly pull his left hand out so he could grab the ball out of the mitt.

Swift at Switching

Abbott learned to switch the glove back and forth between his left hand and right underarm so fast, it was almost as if he had two hands—except better. Some teams tried to test Abbott's fielding skills by having their players bunt a lot. It didn't work. Abbott would run off the mound, field the ball, and throw out the runner just like a two-handed pitcher would. In fact, Abbott became better than all other young pitchers in the state of Michigan. During his senior year in high school, he threw four no-hitters. He also was the starting quarterback on the football team and once threw four touchdown passes in a game.

14

Abbott's most amazing feat in high school was probably batting .427 with seven home runs. Then, as a college pitcher, he posted a record of 26-8 with a 3.03 earned-run average (or ERA). When he was still just a sophomore, Abbott was the winning pitcher for the U.S. National Team as it defeated Cuba in Cuba for the first time in twenty-five years. Abbott also was given the Golden Spikes Award as the top player in college baseball. Then, for his spectacular successes, he was named to the U.S. Olympic Team.

Abbott became one of the stars of the U.S. Olympic squad, posting an 8-1 record with a 2.55 ERA. In the 1988 Summer Games in Seoul, South Korea, he was the winning pitcher in the gold-medal game and led the U.S. to a 5-3 victory over Japan. After the Olympics, he became the first baseball player ever to win the Sullivan Award, which is given to the top amateur athlete in the country. Abbott beat out Olympic gold medal-winning diver Greg Louganis and track star Jackie Joyner-Kersee, probably the best female athlete in the world.

At the ceremony for the Sullivan Award, Abbott got up to accept his honor. He looked over at Louganis and Joyner-Kersee and smiled. "I think they picked the worst athlete up here," he joked. After winning the award, Abbott reported to the California Angels training camp. The Angels had picked him in the first round of the 1988 draft. A lot of teams had wanted Abbott. George Bradley, vice president and director of player development for the New York Yankees, was certain that Abbott was going to be a successful player in the major leagues.

"**W**hen I say success-ful," Bradley explained, "I'm not talk-ing about winning some games in the big leagues. I'm talking about a guy who can win a pennant for you. That's what Jim Abbott can do." The Angels also had high hopes for Abbott. "If there's one thing I've learned about Jim Abbott, it's never say he can't do anything," said Bobby Fontaine, California's director of scouting. The Angels were expecting Abbott to play in the minor leagues in 1989. After all, he was only twenty-one years old and had never pitched an inning of pro baseball. The Angels felt he needed time to get comfortable before he pitched in the majors.

"A Fastball That Really Exploded"

When California's 1989
spring training session began, Abbott
got a chance to show what he could do.
In his first outing, he faced the San
Diego Padres and didn't give up a run in
a couple of innings. "He threw me a
fastball that really exploded," said an
amazed Tim Flannery of the Padres.
"Even the catcher couldn't hold it." Even
though Abbott was probably not going to
make the team, he was the most popular
player in the Angels training camp. He
hadn't even thrown his first pitch as a
pro, yet he had already turned down
three offers to write a book about his
life. A group was also interested in
making a movie about Abbott.

Abbott wasn't concerned with writing books or making movies. He wanted to play major-league baseball, starting in 1989. "All I'm trying to do is pitch the best I can and put myself in a position to be able to make the team," Abbott explained. When spring training ended, the Angels made their decision. Abbott was too good to send to the minor leagues. He made the California roster and would be a starting pitcher for the team—only the tenth pitcher since 1965 to make it to the major leagues without playing a single game in the minors.

Abbott never played in the minors.

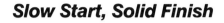

Abbott did not get off to a good start with the Angels. He lost his first four games. But he soon turned things around by winning eight out of nine games. Abbott gave credit for his success to his team. "Dealing with adjustments and attention was easier because the players, manager, and coaches have accepted me as one of the guys from the outset," Abbott said. "No one got worried when I didn't win my first couple of starts. No one panicked when I had an off day. I happened to come to the right situation." Abbott wound up the 1989 season with a 12-12 record and a 3.92 ERA.

"All the questions about him have pretty much been put aside," said former California pitching coach Marcel Lachemann. "Some people worried that he couldn't field bunts. But he's been doing that all his life, and he's good on them. . . . Most important, he has proved he has quality major-league stuff. He has a great breaking [curve] ball. And he seems to throw his best pitches when he's in trouble." Abbott had more trouble in 1990 than in 1989. He struggled to a 10-14 record with a 4.51 ERA. But he put it all together in 1991, finishing with an 18-11 mark and a 2.89 ERA.

30

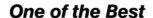

Nobody has any more questions about whether or not the one-handed Jim Abbott can make it in the major leagues. Abbott was traded to the New York Yankees after the 1992 season and is one of the best young pitchers in the game. He actually wishes everyone would forget about his disability. "I don't like to make a big deal out of it," he explained. "There's nothing I want to shout out or tell the public [about having one hand]. I just play baseball. All I ever wanted was a shot to play in the major leagues."

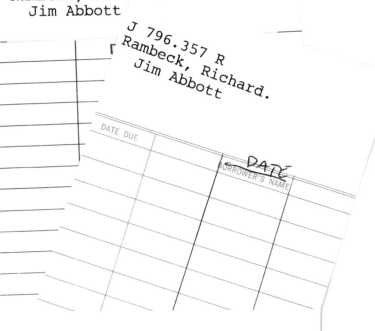

8/00